My Therapist Says...to Color

Ignore Reality and Color Over 50 Designs Because You Can't Even

FROM THE FOUNDERS OF
my therapist says

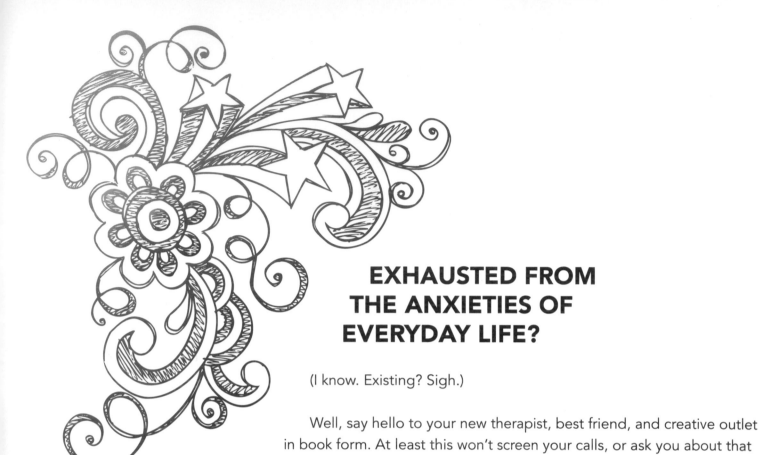

EXHAUSTED FROM THE ANXIETIES OF EVERYDAY LIFE?

(I know. Existing? Sigh.)

Well, say hello to your new therapist, best friend, and creative outlet in book form. At least this won't screen your calls, or ask you about that email you've been putting off ...

My Therapist Says … to Color will bring you the humorous and entertaining commentary you've come to know and love from the team behind my therapist says, with the added bonus of unique images to color using your own creativity and imagination.

Want to color outside the lines? Hone your artistic eye by matching different palettes and color schemes? Then get ready to channel your inner Vincent Van Gogh!

We are about to take you on a kaleidoscopic coloring journey to bring a little bit of that

childlike enjoyment back into your life. With everything else seemingly slipping out of your control, it's nice to find something that can balance and center you while simultaneously indulging your creative side.

Each image, distinct and inspiring, was specifically chosen with the goal of transporting you to complete, internal tranquility. It'll help focus, balance, and calm you during the crazier parts of this non-stop, roller-coaster, exhilarating adventure that we call life.

MAKING ART IS CHEAPER THAN THERAPY...

You should still totally go see a licensed therapist to work out your junk, but here are some ways to channel your woes onto the page through creative expression. It won't evict them entirely, but it'll definitely (probably?) help. If you're not quite the next Frida Kahlo and need a little help with the 'creative expression' bit, coloring in line drawings (like the ones in this coloring book) might just be the perfect form of art for you.

So, if you're feeling particularly crappy and your demons just won't shut up, here's a quick guide on how to work through your issues using this coloring book.

First. Get a margarita. Feelings always go well with a side of indulgence.

Second. Gather all your materials. Color pencils will work best, but if you feel like using high-lighters, markers, crayons, pastels, or the tears of your enemies to color in the pages, all the more power to you. Paint and other wet materials (such as the tears) might wrinkle the page when they dry. It's no biggie if it does, but just so you know.

Third. Put on a podcast, some terrible reality series, your favorite playlist, or the soothing sound of silence to help get you in the coloring zone.

Finally. Find some pages that make you laugh or have compelling images and bring a pop of color to the page.

COLOR TIP

Cool colors (such as blues, greens, and purples) will tell your brain to calm down. Warmer colors (such as red, oranges, and yellows) put your brain in goal-grabbing mode.

In addition, bright colors also tend to have more of a butt-kicking energy, pastel or tinted colors tend to communicate softer energy (think Netflix and nap), while the darker colors usually indicate lower energy, kind of how you feel when you're overthinking something you did when you were 14.

Try gradient coloring. Or color things completely outside of their normal pallet. Maybe you color in the background and leave the image stark white. This is your journey! And your therapist says that there are no right or wrong way to color here. The most important thing when coloring is to figure out which colors you find energizing, and then try to incorporate them into your artwork.

IS TEXTING YOUR EX 42 TIMES
IN A ROW COMING ON TOO STRONG?
ASKING FOR MYSELF.

MY DEPRESSION
AND ANXIETY,
NAME A MORE ICONIC DUO-
I'LL WAIT.

I'M AT THE POINT IN MY LIFE WHERE I REFUSE
TO GO ANYWHERE THAT INVOLVES
PANTS OR WASHING MY HAIR.

YOU SAY I HAVE NO IDEA WHAT
I'M DOING WITH MY LIFE.
I CALL IT BEING MYSTERIOUS.

I WANT SOMEONE WHO I CAN COUNT ON,
SHOWS UP ON TIME, AND FEEDS ME.
SO APPARENTLY, I WANT TO DATE MY DELIVERY DRIVER?

"I'LL HAVE A SALAD, I'M NOT THAT HUNGRY."

GIRLFRIEND CODE FOR:
"I'M GOING TO EAT ALL YOUR FRIES."

MY CONFIDENCE GOES FROM
POTATO TO BEYONCÉ
AT THE SUPER BOWL
WITHIN A MINUTE.

SUNDAY SCARIES ARE JUST EVERYDAY SCARES NOW.

NO SUSAN, THE DRINK I'M HOLDING IS NOT
WHAT MADE ME LATE. IT WAS OBVIOUSLY TRAFFIC.

I HAVE THIS AMAZING ABILITY
TO MAX OUT MY CREDIT CARD
AS SOON AS I SAY
"I WANT TO SAVE MONEY."
I'M LIKE, SO POWERFUL.

USES 'I'M LIVING MY BEST LIFE' AS AN EXCUSE
MAKES LIFE WORSE WITH RECKLESS DECISIONS

I DON'T KNOW WHAT'S
MORE EMPTY:
MY SOUL OR MY WALLET.

MY GOAL IN LIFE IS
TO BE THE GIRL MY
PINTEREST BOARDS
THINK I AM.

WAIT, SO THE "VIBE BEING OFF" ISN'T A GOOD EXCUSE
NOT TO COME INTO WORK? WEIRD.

AND FOR MY NEXT TRICK, I'LL DO NOTHING ALL DAY AND THEN HAVE A PANIC ATTACK ABOUT MY TO-DO LIST.

A FRESH MANICURE
WILL DELUDE ME
INTO THINKING I
HAVE MY LIFE
TOGETHER.

BEING AN ADULT IS ESSENTIALLY JUST CROSSING OFF ONE
THING ON YOUR TO-DO LIST AND THEN REWARDING YOURSELF
BY DOING NOTHING FOR THE REST OF THE DAY.

EARLY BIRDS GET THE WORM,
BUT I NEED
BOTTOMLESS MIMOSAS.

I'M ALWAYS ONE DRINK AWAY
FROM A MENTAL BREAKDOWN.

MY DIET WILL
START TOMORROW,
INDEFINITELY.

I JUST ATE A SALAD FOR LUNCH
AND I STILL DON'T HAVE ABS.
I'M CALLING THE POLICE.

I'M NOT THE SAME PERSON I WAS WHEN I BOUGHT THE HEALTHY FOOD AT THE GROCERY STORE.

ALL I KNOW FOR SURE IS
THAT I'M JUST NOT A
"ONE DRINK"
TYPE OF PERSON.

IMAGINE BEING ABLE
TO ONLY EAT
THE RECOMMENDED
SERVING SIZE?
CAN'T RELATE.

CAN NEVER DECIDE WHAT NETFLIX SHOW TO WATCH.
I'M PROCRASTINATING MY PROCRASTINATING.

MY LIFE IS BASICALLY JUST A NEVER-ENDING CYCLE
OF WANTING SOMETHING SWEET AFTER SALTY,
AND SALTY AFTER SWEET.

AT WHAT AGE DO I STOP ASKING MY MOM TO MAKE MY APPOINTMENTS FOR ME? NEVER, RIGHT? RIGHT.

ME: THIS IS THE YEAR I'M GOING TO GET MY LIFE TOGETHER.
NARRATOR: SHE SAYS THAT EVERY YEAR....

I WISH I SPENT AS MUCH TIME TRYING TO GET MY LIFE TOGETHER AS I DO PICKING A SHOW ON NETFLIX.

NO 90S BABY CAN DO ALL 5:
GET TO WORK ON TIME WITH A COFFEE,
DO THEIR OWN TAXES, MAINTAIN SEROTONIN LEVELS,
RECOVER AFTER DRINKING, AND TEXT BACK.

MY NIGHTLY ROUTINE CONSISTS OF REMEMBERING
AWKWARD THINGS I SAID IN 2005.

THE BEST PART
ABOUT BEING SINGLE
IS SLEEPING
DIAGONALLY.

NEED A NIGHT CREAM THAT HIDES
THE FACT THAT I ALWAYS STAY UP WATCHING
"JUST ONE MORE EPISODE."

SOME DAYS THE MOST PRODUCTIVE THING I DO IS TAKE OFF MY DAYTIME PAJAMAS AND PUT ON MY NIGHTTIME PAJAMAS.

THERE'S NO BETTER FEELING
THAN THE NAP YOU TAKE
AFTER DAY DRINKING.
THIS IS NOT UP FOR DEBATE.
THANK YOU FOR COMING TO
MY TED TALK.

MY OUTFIT TODAY CAN
BE BEST DESCRIBED AS
"I DIDN'T THINK I WAS
GETTING OUT OF THE CAR."

DUE TO

PERSONAL

REASONS,

I WILL BE

DRINKING

AT 9 AM.

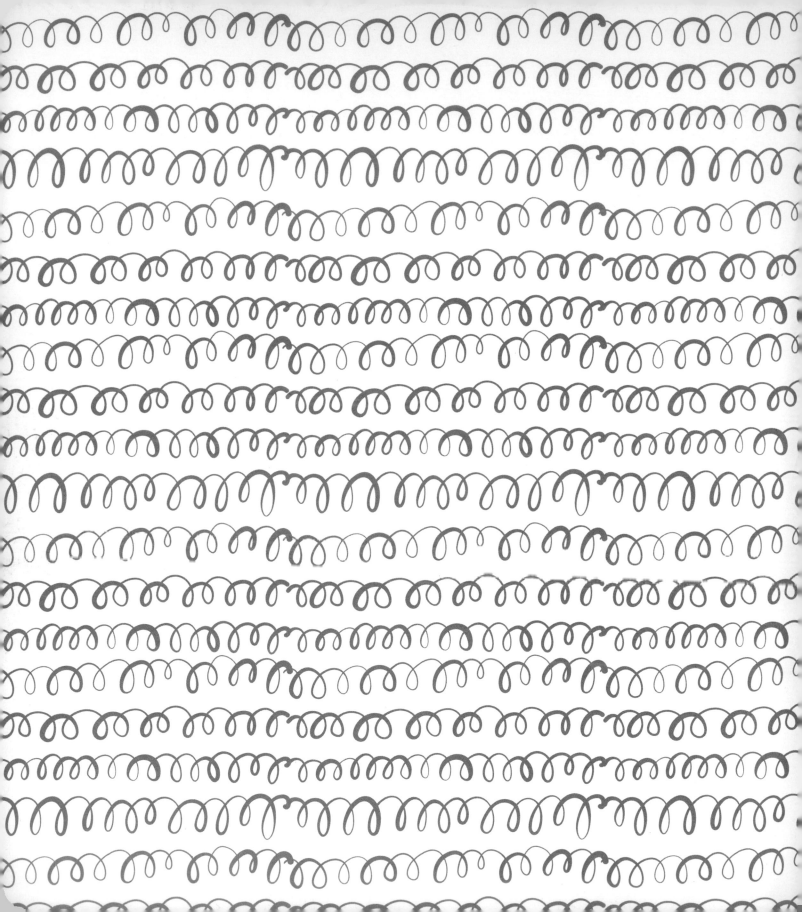

WAKES UP AND OPENS EYES I'M JUST **SO** READY FOR BED.

STILL CONFUSED
HOW PEOPLE
FORGET TO EAT
WHEN ALL I DO IS
THINK ABOUT FOOD.

I'M EITHER BEING ANNOYING OR ANNOYED. THERE'S NO IN BETWEEN.

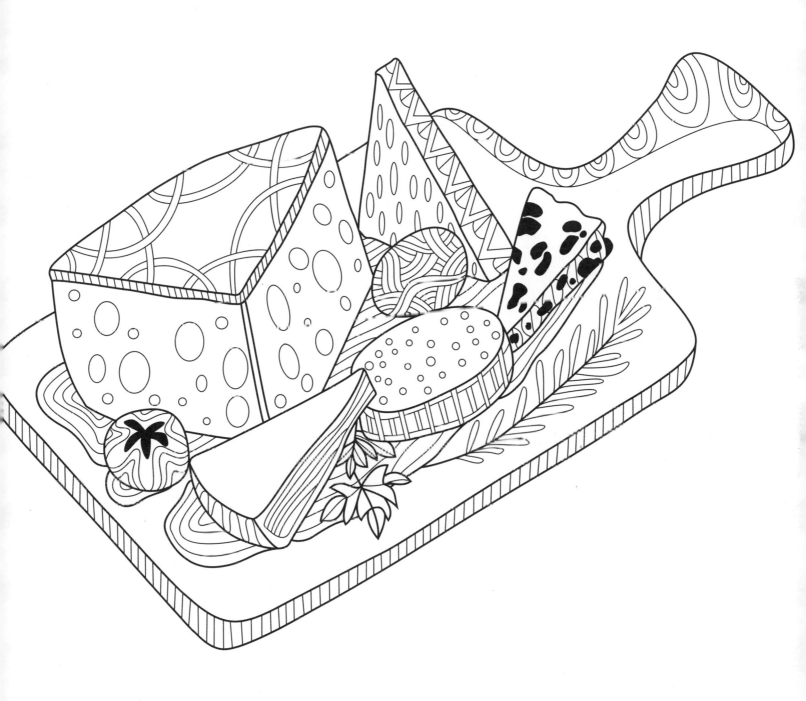

ALL MY FRIENDSHIPS ARE HELD TOGETHER BY CHEESE
AND MUTUAL HATRED.

WHEN YOU'RE IN A
BAD MOOD AND
SOMEONE SAYS
"CHEER UP,"
THANKS SUSAN,
NEVER THOUGHT OF
THAT. I'M FINE NOW,
HAHA, I LOVE LIFE.

I DON'T KNOW WHO NEEDS TO HEAR THIS
BUT JUST ORDER THE FRIES OVER THE SALAD.

ON A SCALE OF 1 TO DOING A MAKEUP TUTORIAL
TO SIT AT HOME ALONE—HOW BORED ARE YOU?

IT'S LISTEN-TO-SAD-MUSIC-WHEN
I'M-ALREADY-SAD O'CLOCK.

I LOVE DRUNK ME,
BUT I DON'T TRUST HER.

IF YOU SEE ME WEARING THE SAME SWEATPANTS THREE DAYS IN A ROW, MIND YOUR BUSINESS.

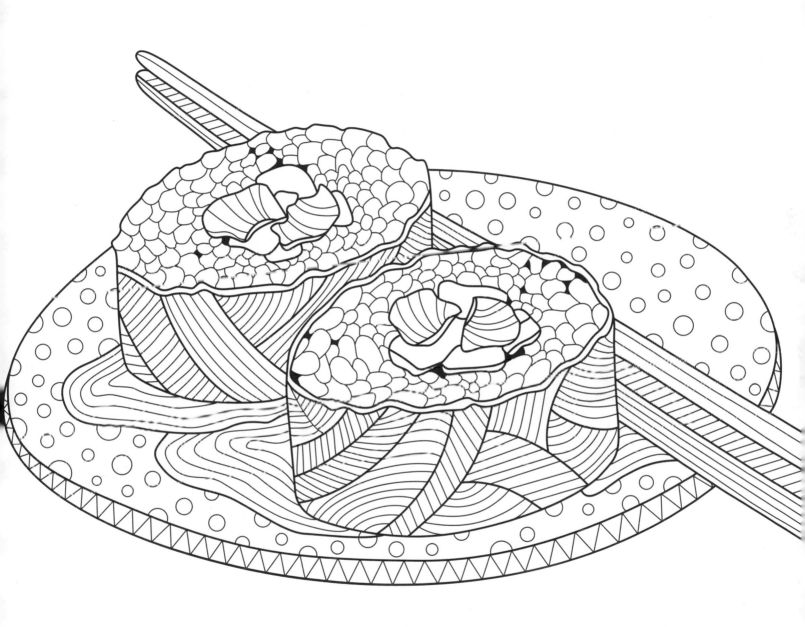

MY RESTING BITCH FACE IS REALLY JUST ME THINKING
HARD ABOUT WHAT I'M HAVING FOR DINNER.

First published in 2020 by Rock Point, an imprint of The Quarto Group,
142 West 36th Street, 4th Floor, New York, NY 10018 USA
T (212) 779-4972 F (212) 779-6058 www.QuartoKnows.com

Rock Point titles are also available at discount for retail, wholesale, promotional, and bulk purchase. For details, contact the Special Sales Manager by email at specialsales@quarto.com or by mail at The Quarto Group, Attn: Special Sales Manager, 100 Cummings Center Suite 265D, Beverly, MA 01915 USA.

10 9 8 7 6 5

ISBN: 978-1-63106-745-7

Publisher: Rage Kindelsperger
Creative Director: Laura Drew
Managing Editor: Cara Donaldson
Project Editor: Leeann Moreau
Cover & Interior Design: Laura Drew

Printed in China